THE RESPIRATORY SYSTEM

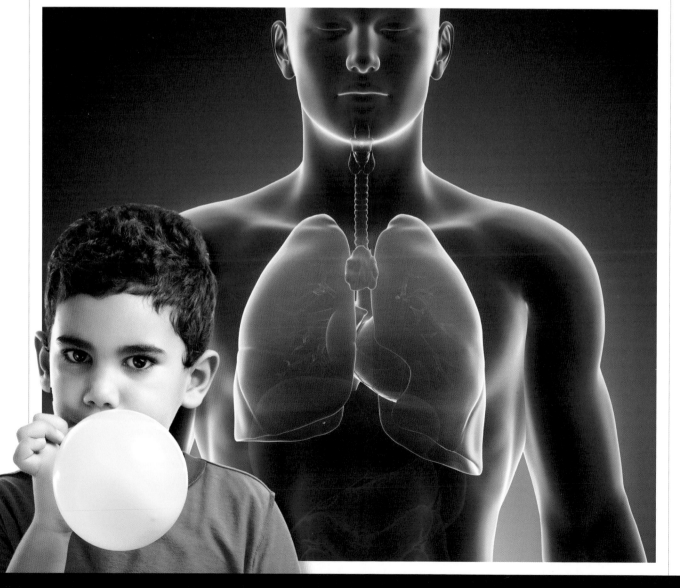

BY SUSAN H. GRAY

Published by The Child's World®
1980 Lookout Drive • Mankato, MN 56003-1705
800-599-READ • www.childsworld.com

Acknowledgments
The Child's World®: Mary Berendes, Publishing Director
Red Line Editorial: Editorial direction
The Design Lab: Design
Amnet: Production

Content Consultant: R. John Solaro, Ph.D., Distinguished University
Professor and Head, Department of Physiology and Biophysics,
University of Illinois Chicago

Photographs ©: Shutterstock Images, cover (foreground),
1 (foreground), 19; CLIPAREA/Custom Media/Shutterstock
Images, cover (background), 1 (background); Val Thoermer/
Shutterstock Images, 4; Alila Medical Media/Shutterstock
Images, 7, 15; Patrick Foto/Shutterstock Images, 9; Gino's
Photos/iStockphoto, 11; Sebastian Kaulitzki/Shutterstock
Images, 13; iStockphoto/Thinkstock, 16, 20

ISBN 9781626873384
LCCN 2014930675

Printed in the United States of America
Mankato, MN
July, 2014
PA02221

ABOUT THE AUTHOR

Susan H. Gray has a bachelor's and a master's degree in zoology. In her 25 years as an author, she has written many medical articles, grant proposals, and children's books. Ms. Gray and her husband, Michael, live in Cabot, Arkansas.

TABLE OF CONTENTS

CHAPTER 1

Samantha Sings!

I t was Samantha's turn to sing. The music started, and Samantha took a long, deep breath.

Air rushed into her nose and mouth. It flowed through **passages** in her skull. Then it moved down

Your respiratory system helps you breathe, speak, and sing.

into her throat. Air slipped between flaps of tissue in her throat called **vocal cords**, then into her chest. It flowed into two tubes. One led to the right lung and the other led to the left. The air moved deeper and deeper into her lungs. It had reached the little air pockets. Millions of the pockets inflated.

Oxygen in the pockets seeped into the nearby blood vessels. Blood picked up the oxygen and carried it through Samantha's body. Oxygen helped keep all of her tissues working. Her brain could think about the music. Her ears could hear the piano.

Samantha's vocal cords moved close together. She opened her mouth to sing the first note. Air from her lungs pushed against the vocal cords. The cords vibrated together, and the note began to come out. Samantha's respiratory system was helping her.

CHAPTER 2

What Is the Respiratory System?

The word respiratory comes from a Latin word meaning "to breathe." The respiratory system has to do with breathing. It includes more than the lungs. It involves all of the tubes and air **sacs** that fill up and empty as a person breathes. Muscles help **expand** the lungs and move air in and out of the lungs. Nerves in the brain automatically make the muscles work.

The respiratory system includes the nose, mouth, windpipe, voice box, and lungs. Most people do not notice when these organs are working. But each organ plays a big part in breathing.

Each time a person breathes in, or inhales, air passes through the nose or mouth. From there, the air moves through the pharynx. The pharynx is the area in the upper part of the throat. Air then moves

The Respiratory System

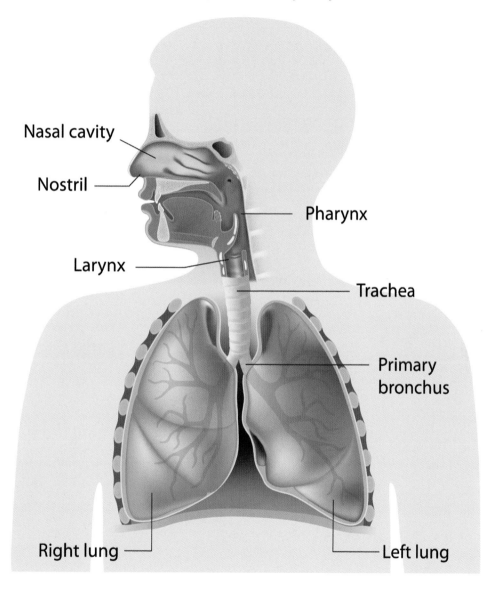

Nasal cavity

Nostril

Larynx

Right lung

Pharynx

Trachea

Primary bronchus

Left lung

There are many parts to the respiratory system.

through the voice box and down the windpipe, or trachea. This is a tube that is about as wide as a garden hose. In an adult, it is about 4.5 inches (11 cm) long.

The bottom of the trachea splits into two branches. One branch leads to the right lung. The other leads to the left lung. Each branch is called a bronchus. The two branches together are called bronchi. Each bronchus splits into smaller and smaller branches. The branches become so small they can barely be seen. At the ends of the tiniest branches are air sacs called alveoli. The alveoli have moist, thin, delicate walls. Tiny blood vessels wrap around the outside of each sac.

The bronchi, their branches, and millions of alveoli make up the lungs. The lungs are in the chest, just behind the ribs. The heart sits right between them. Lungs are very spongy organs. They do

DID YOU KNOW?
The average person has about 600 million alveoli.

not weigh very much. This is because they are full of so many air sacs.

When a person breathes, some air goes down the left bronchus and some goes down the right one. Air keeps moving through all the branches until it reaches the alveoli. Most of the alveoli fill up with air. The chest and ribs expand as this happens. Then the chest and ribs relax. Air moves from the alveoli, back through all the tubes, and out through the mouth or nose.

You don't have to think about breathing all the time, especially when you're playing with friends.

CHAPTER 3

What Is the Voice Box?

At the top of the trachea is a structure called the voice box, or larynx. It is used in speaking, singing, and making other sounds.

Inside the larynx are the vocal cords. They are little folds of soft tissue. When you are breathing, these folds move apart. This allows air to move freely through the voice box.

Usually you inhale before speaking. When you are ready to talk, the folds in the larynx move together. As you exhale, air from your lungs makes the folds vibrate. The **vibration** makes a sound.

DID YOU KNOW?

Some people have a big Adam's apple. This is a bump that often sticks out in the front of the neck. The Adam's apple is really a part of the voice box.

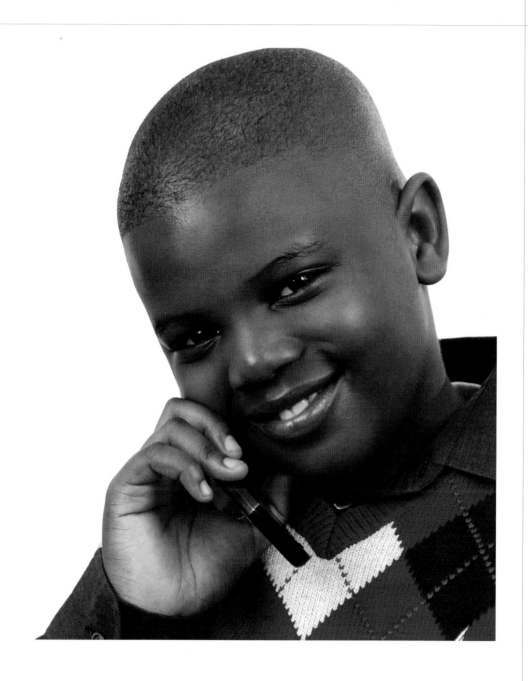

You use the roof of your mouth and your lips, tongue, and teeth to turn the sounds into words.

CHAPTER 4

Why Do You Breathe?

Breathing is very important. After all, you do it all the time. You breathe for two main reasons. Breathing helps your tissues get the oxygen they need. You also breathe so your tissues can get rid of a waste gas called **carbon dioxide**.

Air is made up of several different gases. The main gas is nitrogen. Almost four-fifths of the air is made up of this gas. Oxygen makes up about one-fifth of the air. The rest of the air is made up of many gases in very small amounts, including carbon dioxide.

The body's tissues and organs all need oxygen to work properly. The heart cannot beat without

DID YOU KNOW?
Asthma is a lung condition common in children. It is caused when the lungs are overly sensitive to irritants. The airways react to these things by tightening and narrowing, making it very difficult to breathe.

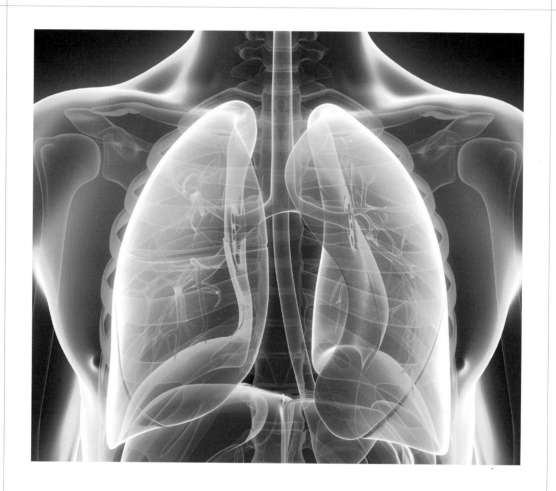

oxygen. The brain cannot think without it. Arm and leg muscles cannot move unless they get oxygen.

As tissues and organs do their work, they create waste materials. One of these is carbon dioxide. This gas must be removed so tissues can keep working. The job of the respiratory system is to bring in oxygen and get rid of the carbon dioxide.

When you breathe in, your lungs take in air.

CHAPTER 5

What Does the Blood Do?

The respiratory system is in your head, neck, and chest. But how does oxygen travel to the rest of your body?

The lungs do not actually take oxygen to the tissues. And they do not take carbon dioxide away from them. These are jobs for the blood. Special cells in the blood are built just for carrying these gases.

Blood is always on the move. It moves through the tiny vessels next to the alveoli, which are in the lungs. It moves to the heart. The heart pumps blood out to the body's tissues. It pumps blood all throughout the body. Blood comes back to the heart and is pumped to the lungs. It moves past the alveoli again. Over and over, all day long, blood makes this trip.

Structure of an Alveolus

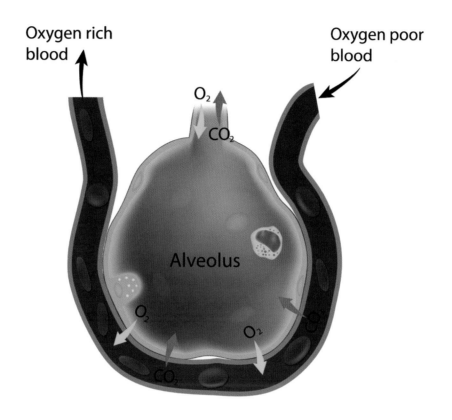

Oxygen rich blood

Oxygen poor blood

O_2

CO_2

Alveolus

O_2

O_2

CO_2

Each time you breathe in, your lungs take in nitrogen, oxygen, and other gases in the air. These gases fill your lungs and **inflate** the alveoli. Blood moving alongside the alveoli picks up the oxygen. Loaded with oxygen, blood travels to the heart. The heart pumps it out to the rest of the body.

Alveoli are where the exchange of oxygen and carbon dioxide takes place.

The heart pumps blood to every single tissue and organ. When blood reaches the tissues, oxygen leaves the blood. It goes right into the tissues so they can keep working.

Then carbon dioxide moves from the tissues into the blood. As the blood keeps moving, it hauls the carbon dioxide away. Soon this blood reaches the heart. The heart pumps it right to the lungs. Again, blood goes into the tiny vessels wrapped

The heart pumps blood all the way up to the eyelids before pumping it through the lungs!

around the alveoli. Then carbon dioxide moves out of the blood and into the alveoli. Carbon dioxide leaves the lungs when you breathe out. Then the blood picks up more inhaled oxygen and heads back to the heart.

The lungs, heart, and blood all work together. They make sure every single body part gets oxygen. They also make sure carbon dioxide gets carried away.

CHAPTER 6

Some Breathing Problems

Sometimes the respiratory system does not work properly. This is often because the lungs get an infection. Everyone catches the common cold at some time. Colds are caused by more than 200 different kinds of viruses. You often have a sore throat, a cough, and a runny nose. You usually do not have a fever.

A few viruses cause a particular kind of infection. These are the flu viruses. The real name for the flu is influenza. The influenza virus comes in through the nose or mouth. It attacks the nose, throat, and lungs. A person with the flu seems to have a cold but also has a fever.

The common cold and the flu are very contagious diseases. That means they spread easily from person to person. When an infected person sneezes or coughs, the virus spews out into the air. Someone else breathes in the virus. Soon, they have the disease, too.

When you sneeze, germs may fly into the air where someone else can breathe them in.

Other things can cause the respiratory system to work poorly. Smoking is the worst thing for the lungs. Breathing polluted air is also harmful. After years of smoking or breathing dirty air, people can get lung cancer. They feel chest pain and they cough a lot. They also feel as though they are not getting enough air.

Exercising and playing with friends will help keep your lungs healthy.

You can keep your lungs healthy by exercising and by not smoking. A healthy respiratory system can work fine for a lifetime. It cleans the air coming into the body. It draws

oxygen into the blood. It gets rid of carbon dioxide. With each breath, it does all of these jobs. And every day, an adult takes more than 20,000 breaths. The respiratory system never rests. It does an incredible job.

GLOSSARY

carbon dioxide (KAR-buhn dye-OK-side) Carbon dioxide is a gas produced when people and animals breathe out. Breathing gets rid of carbon dioxide in the body.

expand (ek-SPAND) To expand is to increase in size, range, or amount. Muscles help expand the lungs.

inflate (in-FLATE) To inflate is to add air or gas to something and make it larger. Gases fill the lungs and inflate the alveoli.

passages (PASS-uh-jez) Passages are long, narrow spaces that connect one place to another. Air flows through passages in the body.

sacs (SAKS) Sacs are parts inside the body that are shaped like bags and usually contain liquid or air. Alveoli are tiny air sacs.

vibration (vye-BRA-shuhn) Vibration is a continuous shaking movement. The vibration in your lungs makes sounds.

vocal cords (VOH-kol KORDS) Vocal cords are thin pieces of folded tissue in your throat that help you make sounds with your voice. The vocal cords are inside the larynx.

LEARN MORE

BOOKS

Gardner, Jane P. *Take a Closer Look at Your Lungs.* Mankato, MN: The Child's World, 2014.

Manolis, Kay. *The Respiratory System.* Minneapolis: Bellwether Media, 2009.

VanVoorst, Jenny Fretland. *Take a Closer Look at Your Nose.* Mankato, MN: The Child's World, 2014.

WEB SITES

Visit our Web site for links about the respiratory system:

childsworld.com/links

Note to Parents, Teachers, and Librarians: We routinely verify our Web links to make sure they are safe and active sites. So encourage your readers to check them out!

INDEX